Tessa Ransford was born in India, educated in Scotland and has lived all her adult life in Scotland, apart from eight years working in Pakistan in the 1960s. She was founder of the Scottish Poetry Library, which she directed from 1984-1999, founder/organiser of the School of Poets poetry workshop (1981-1999) and was editor of *Lines Review* poetry magazine from 1988 until its final issue in 1998. She now works as a freelance poetry adviser and practitioner, and has been attached as Royal Literary Fund Fellow to the Centre for Human Ecology in Edinburgh. In 2000 she set up the Callum Macdonald Memorial Award to encourage the publication of poetry pamphlets, and is currently President of International PEN's Scottish Centre. She was awarded an O.B.E. for her services to the Scottish Poetry Library in 2000, and an honorary doctorate from the University of Paisley in 2003.

D1728747

*Also by Tessa Ransford:*

*Light of the Mind*, Ramsay Head Press 1980
*Fools and Angels*, Ramsay Head Press 1984
*Shadows from the Greater Hill*, Ramsay Head Press 1987
*A Dancing Innocence*, Macdonald Publishers, Edinburgh 1988
*Seven Valleys*, Ramsay Head Press 1991
*Medusa Dozen and Other Poems*, Ramsay Head Press 1994
*Scottish Selection*, Akros Publications 1998 (reissued 2001)
*When it works it feels like Play*, Ramsay Head Press 1998
*Indian Selection*, Akros Publications 2000
*Natural Selection*, Akros Publications 2001
*Noteworthy Selection*, Akros Publications 2002

# Tessa Ransford
### (editor/translator)

*To dear Anette,*
*In memory of our Time out of*
*Time!*
*love from Tessa*

# The Nightingale Question

## *Five Poets from Saxony*

### Portraits & photographs by
### Joyce Gunn-Cairns

### Shearsman Books
### 2004

First published in the United Kingdom in 2004 by
Shearsman Books,
58 Velwell Road,
Exeter EX4 4LD

http://www.shearsman.com/

ISBN 0-907562-52-3

Shearsman Books thanks the following publishers & copyright-holders for their permission to reprint the original poems and translations in this volume:

Insel Verlag, Frankfurt and Leipzig, for five poems taken from Thomas Rosenlöcher: *Am Wegrand steht Apollo. Wiepersdorfer Tagebuch. Gedichte. Mit Zeichnungen von Dieter Goltzsche*, IB 1224, copyright © 2001, Insel Verlag;

Ammann Verlag & Co., Zürich, Switzerland, for five poems by Wulf Kirsten, copyright © 2004 by Ammann Verlag & Co.;

Andreas Reimann and Connewitzer Verlagsbuchhandlung, Leipzig, for two poems from the volume *Das Sonettarium*, copyright © 1995, Andreas Reimann and Connewitzer Verlagsbuchhandlung; Andreas Reimann & Verlag Die Scheune, Dresden, for two poems from *Der Olivenspiegel*, copyright © 2003, Verlag die Scheune; Andreas Reimann for the poems 'Widerrufliche Ermutigung' and 'Utopia', copyright © 2004 by Andreas Reimann;

Elmar Schenkel for permission to reproduce four texts from the books *Leipziger Passagen* (Verlag Reiner Brouwer, Stuttgart, 1996), copyright © 1996, Verlag Reiner Brouwer, and *Blauverschiebung. Gedichte.* (Flugasche-Verlag, Reiner Brouwer, Stuttgart, 1992), copyright © 1992 by Flugasche-Verlag (Reiner Brouwer).

Uta Mauersberger for permission to reprint six poems, copyright © 2004 by Uta Mauersberger.

*Acknowledgements*

Shearsman Books thanks Hugh Anderson, Eric Wishart, and a further anonymous donor for their assistance with this publication, which has enabled it to appear on schedule.

Some of these translations have appeared in earlier versions in the following magazines, to whose editors grateful acknowledgement is made: *Northwords, Oasis.*

# CONTENTS

# Introduction

I started working on the poetry of the German Democratic Republic (East Germany) in the 1980s, when I read work by young GDR authors and thought it some of the most exciting contemporary poetry being written in Europe. There was an extraordinary charge about these poems, as if they were being written under some enormous pressure, and came to the reader with an accumulated weight of experience denied or silenced. Poetry was the place where the true reality of life in the GDR found a voice. It is a truism to say that in poetry every word matters, but in these poems every word mattered in a special way. It was being uttered against the backdrop of a silence which threatened to extinguish it completely. But also it was being written, very often, as a form of existential necessity. And the language was very finely tuned too. It walked a kind of tightrope – hoping to evade the censors, but at the same time to reach a reading public skilled at reading between the lines, and hungry to see its own experience and frustration articulated.

Some of those poets I read back then feature in this anthology, but the circumstances in which we read them have changed irrevocably. The sentry boxes and barbed wire are long gone. The oppressive mechanisms of state and censorship, with which they once had to do battle, no longer impinge on their writing. Even their country, and the extraordinary events of 1989, are just history to many of the young people that I teach. East Germany – a city divided by a Wall, a country fenced-off, a velvet revolution? Not many European poets go through such momentous changes in their lives: to have all the circumstances of their existence changed in one fell swoop, to find themselves writing in a very different world, with very different demands. Suddenly they find themselves within a market place where they are free to write as they wish, but where there are few people to listen. But if few poets live through such changes, nor do many poems. Today these poems are read in different ways, with different experiences and knowledge. The morbid curiosity of Western readers, most easily visible in the crowds who used to stand on the platform on the Western side of the Berlin Wall, has gone. But also gone is what some called the 'dissident bonus' with which poems from the East were read. The poems stand now more naked than ever but precisely because of this they can at last be judged on their own merits.

Something curious happened with time in 1989. In German one speaks of 1989 as the 'Wendezeit' [the time of revolution], but it was also a 'Zeitwende' [revolution in time], when a long period of stagnation came to an end in a sudden telescoping of experience and change. Many were left stranded by this epochal shift. Their poems about a country which no longer exists, their memories of ways of living, their narratives of change and adaptation all might seem impossibly foreign even at such a short distance. And doubly so to a reader in this country, so far from such historical events, or the poetic traditions in which the poems stand. Yet the poems collected here speak to us urgently and clearly, giving us a window onto lives which are both strange but also familiar.

Poems from Eastern Europe are commonly thought of as epigrammatic and bleak – and, for all their high moral tone, sometimes bordering on the obscure. The poems here cheat those expectations. For all the burden of experience they carry, they are also much more concerned to explore ways of saying. Readers might be surprised to see the humour of very many of the poems, which varies from a gentle whimsy to a dark and caustic tone. There are references to myths and fairytales and even a surreal twist to some of the poems. Even those poems written explicitly out of the most difficult personal situations hold that experience at arm's length and offer a sly wink.

The poets collected here are inheritors of a very special tradition within GDR poetry. A loose grouping of older poets, most of whom lived around Leipzig, became known as the 'Sächsische Dichterschule' [The Saxon School of Poetry]. They were poets who mainly came to prominence in the 1960s and studied for the most part under the mentor Georg Maurer at the J.R. Becher Institute for Literature in Leipzig. Now they are some of the most distinguished poets in the united Germany: Volker Braun, Sarah Kirsch, Karl Mickel, Heinz Czechowski. Their poetry was distinctive in many ways and brought the region around Leipzig powerfully to bear as a direct counter-pole to the excitement of Berlin. It would be wrong to overemphasise this aspect though. Their label had as much to do with parodying historical schools of poetry, and also the schoolmasterly overtones of the socialist realist notion of an apprenticeship in poetry, as with any geographical aspect. But most important was a kind of fellow-feeling which established their identity on the poetical map. The poets gathered here share many of the same traits – the geographical centre, the interest in landscape, and some indeed studied at the Leipzig Institute. If this grouping is much looser, one can still trace a network of affinities and shared concerns. It is striking for example that the Romantic tradition which was such a vital touchstone for many poets in the GDR still makes its mark. Thomas Rosenlöcher, for example, turns to the graves of Bettina and Achim von Arnim in several poems: 'a stone's throw away' from the cars of the living. It seems that they have been forgotten in the rush of progress:

> There is no remembering.
> Only these conflicting times.
> One step does not know the next.

History can perhaps bide its time: 'But the woods are patient as iron'. And there are dignified possibilities in what has apparently been lost in the throng:

> Only the forgotten can again be
> what they were, to go on becoming.

Leipzig itself is a tangible presence in the poems of almost all the poets, both the Leipzig of 1989 with its demonstrations: 'A moment is knocking on the gate of history' (Elmar Schenkel), but also the long disappointment that came after. This is clearest in a remarkable sequence of poems by Uta Mauersberger. These poems are entitled 'Leipzig', with one written every year in September between 1989 and 1993. It is like watching a time-lapse film. The exuberant hope of the first poem is caught in a wonderfully surreal imagery – 'Now we want / to batter through doors to reach the impossible'. However, this is replaced by a grim realisation that the hopes of that magical moment will not be realised. The fairy-tale atmosphere of the earlier poems becomes darker and the syntax disintegrates to a stuttering silence. Schenkel's own response in his 'Leipziger Passagen' is quite different. These bitterly ironic prose-poems deconstruct the regime that has passed, and the stultifying legacy that remains, with satirical verve.

Wulf Kirsten's poems might seem at first to be removed from that reality and yet their concerns are in many ways broader. The surface play of humour, fairy-tale and myth gives way to sudden insights into an even darker legacy. His gentle insights into the natural world recede to reveal the long shadow of the Third Reich. The novelist Martin Walser said of Kirsten's language that 'he lives as if barefoot'. Notwithstanding their raw sensitivity and exquisite sound textures, his poems are political in their own way, dragging layers of history out of oblivion.

Andreas Reimann also writes against forgetting. But his tone is that of a bitter gallows humour. Thomas Rosenlöcher, for example, treats mortality with whimsical detachment in 'Bells':

No bad thought that an iron clapper
will still keep you in mind for two hours
after you die.

The same theme receives a bleakly ironic treatment at the hands of Reimann, as his own scarred family history is recapitulated in 'Uncalled for Encouragement'. But the same concerns give way to a more general lament in 'Utopia'. Here an ironic vision of the future (with echoes of Brecht) imagines nature reasserting itself over the oppressive structures of humankind until:

And the whole of nature
            will presumably
                        notice our disappearance,
if at all,
with the utmost relief.

Reimann is the writer most explicitly concerned with poetry itself. His pointed sonnets turn also to myth and the new Germany, but with profound questions to ask of the possibilities for poetry in the current 'altogether purposeless' world. That all of the poets represented here see poetry as a means of intervening in the world is clear. That their language brings that commitment vividly to life is also clear. Tessa Ransford's lucid and tactful translations themselves testify to the energy and honesty of the work. But her own poems included here also bear witness to the possibilities of poetry to reach accross cultures and experiences and make something happen:

> We came here to translate
> and have been ourselves translated.
> We came here to portray
> and have seen ourselves portrayed.

Karen Leeder, 2004

Long ago, when I was a student at Edinburgh University, the Professor of German was Eudo C. Mason. He loved poetry and enthused his students to do the same. He used to rave about Leipzig, where he had studied, and all my life I retained a certain 'Sehnsucht' for Leipzig, hoping I might one day visit that city of literature and music. This was fostered by my friend Dr Karin MacPherson of Edinburgh University's German Department, who has for years encouraged and helped my efforts at translating German poetry. I would also like to thank Dr Howard Gaskill, Hon. Fellow in German, University of Edinburgh, for his support and advice, especially with Wulf Kirsten's poems.

I did visit Leipzig in summer 2000 and called on my friend Dr. Elmar Schenkel, professor in the Department of Anglistik in the university. We had first met in 1990 at Blaubeuren near Tübingen and had kept up a correspondence since, including Elmar's contributing from time to time to *Lines Review*, the magazine of which I was editor. In 1991 in *Lines Review* number 119 I had produced a German issue, with poets from former East and West Germany appearing together in translations by Michael Hamburger, Raymond Hargreaves and Michael Hulse. Elmar Schenkel and Wulf Kirsten were among those poets. In the same year I organised a reading at the Edinburgh Festival for two of the poets.

Forward now to summer 2001, when, to my surprise and without having applied for it, I was awarded a Travelling Scholarship by the Society of Authors. I did not spend long wondering where I would go, but decided it had to be Leipzig. I imagined the pleasure of living there for a few weeks and getting to know some of the poets. Accordingly I wrote to Elmar, to Ingrid Sonntag of Die Freie Akademie der Kunst, to the Kulturamt and to the British Council. Eventually a visit was planned for the following Spring and rooms were booked for me in the University Guesthouse overlooking the Nikolai Platz, right in the centre of the city. The Edinburgh artist Joyce Gunn-Cairns was able to join me on the project, thanks to a grant from the Scottish Arts Council. She made portrait-sketches of the poets and photographed them, while also working on other drawings inspired by Leipzig. Joyce's enthusiasm, artistic skill and fluent German contributed significantly to the pleasure and success of the project.

During my stay I met several poets and began to translate some of their poems. The first one I discovered was Thomas Rosenlöcher, who was giving a reading in a bookshop in Leipzig during the Buchmesse. The little shop was crammed with young people and Rosenlöcher was obviously a brilliant poet and performer of his work. I asked him if I might visit him and he agreed, although it meant meeting in Dresden (thirty miles drive for him and a train journey for me). I wanted to visit Dresden, which I hadn't managed to do during the 2000 trip. I began to translate some of Rosenlöcher's poems from his new book, *Am Wegrand steht Apollo* and by the time we met in a Dresden café I had drafts to show him and go over with him, asking him what this or that meant. What kind of bird was a 'Sprosser'? The second poet I met was Andreas Reimann. I was immediately impressed by his emotional poetry, heart-wringing and tragic, beautifully written. The story of his life was harrowing and kept me from sleeping for several nights. I was all the more inspired to try to do justice to his exquisite sonnets and searing free verse poems. We met at his home the first time and then again in a Leipzig café, which he regularly frequents.

The third poet I met was Uta Mauersberger, a lively, intelligent, modern poet with a sequence of poems called 'Leipzig' written each year since *Die Wende*. I found Uta warm and interesting. However she was suffering from marginalisation due to her having been involved with the Stasi at one point, in order to save her brother, who had tried to escape abroad.

The fourth poet I met was Wulf Kirsten. He invited me to Weimar and was most kind and hospitable. He told me about Weimar and its compromised situation over Buchenwald. He told me some of the terrible stories of what happened both under the Nazis and the Communists. I had visited Weimar in 2000 and had found myself at the Ernst Thälmann Renault Garage, so had learnt then about his fate. These things, together with my own long-harboured reverence for Goethe and Schiller, made Weimar a place of especial importance.

Of course Elmar was the fifth, or the first in fact. I knew him to be extraordinarily intelligent and wide-ranging in his scope. It seems there is no language, culture, country or subject about which Elmar does not know a good deal and also is able to make connections between them. I am looking forward to his visiting Scotland and experiencing some aspects of our 'democratic intellect'.

Apart from the poets, I was befriended by The British Council, and by Alexandria, Andrea, Stefan, Dietmar, Reinhild, Ingrid, Sibille and Elena in Leipzig.

The theme that seemed to emerge from conversations and the poetry itself was one of forgetting and remembering, linked as well to dying and re-incarnating. Not only the experience of individuals and communities, but the very buildings and cities themselves have suffered loss and destruction, pain and oppression throughout the twentieth century. The new century and 'Die Wende', the re-uniting of Germany, have given the opportunity for new beginnings and new hope. But the weight of sorrow from the past is always there and the future is not rosy, with unemployment high and the initial investment from the West beginning to wane. In due course the theme that came to me was one of emergence and re-mergence, as it were a cyclical form of renewal and hope, not ignoring what is painful but emerging from it strengthened. The nearest German equivalents: *auftauchen und eintauchen*, seem also appropriate, especially as *eintauchen* is a word used for deep textual analysis.

In these poems I offer texts and textures of various dimensions: linguistic, cultural, personal and, I hope, allowing new depths of understanding and friendship to emerge and remerge between Edinburgh and Leipzig, Scotland and Saxony.

I warmly thanks those who made this book possible: Karen Leeder for her interesting introduction, Joyce Gunn-Cairns for her immense contribution throughout the project and Rose O'Connor for professional artwork design. I am most grateful to Shearsman Books' editor, Tony Frazer, for the care he has taken over this book, making it a worthy tribute to these remarkable poets.

Tessa Ransford, 2004.

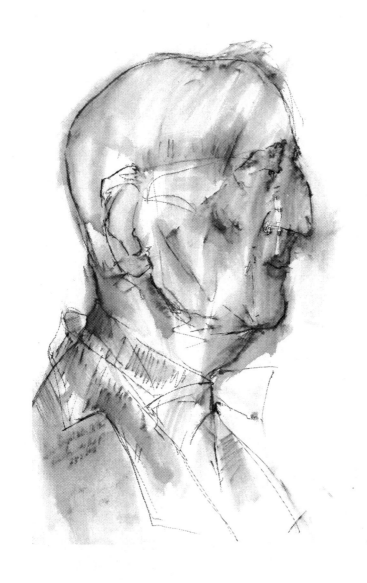

## TESSA RANSFORD

### *The Angel of Leipzig*

'O it's him' they said, but
nobody knew his name and
there he stood, leaning against the wall
at a ceremony in the old Rathaus
suited in black, austere and dignified
his bald head and roman nose in profile
like some great hawk, some Brutus
that waits in the wings for
who knows what act of honour.

Or perhaps he attends events
to beatify and mark their emergence
from the implicate order of things
in order to have their day. 'Often'
they say, 'he brings a rose or a candle.'

Rosicrucian or peregrine, or spirit
made manifest by some crucial
conjunction of deadly truth
with living beauty, in ways
that demand such presence:

executioner or saviour, recording
he is recorded, the black and white angel
of Leipzig.

# WULF KIRSTEN

Wulf Kirsten was born in 1934 near Meissen, Saxony. After his apprenticeship he held various jobs in the 1950s, but attended the Workers' and Peasants' Faculty in Leipzig as a mature student from 1957-1960 where he obtained his Abitur (high school graduation certificate). Thereafter he studied to be a teacher. Since 1965 he has lived in Weimar and worked as an Editor at the Aufbau-Verlag (Berlin and Weimar) until 1987. Since 1987 he has been a freelance writer. He has been awarded numerous prizes including the Marie-Luise Kaschnitz Prize (2000) and the Schiller Ring (2002).

Amongst his many publications are the poetry collections *Wettersturz* (*Sudden Fall in Temperature*, 1999) and *Stimmenschotter* (*Voice Ballast*, 1993, both Ammann Verlag, Zürich); the novel *Die Prinzessin im Krautgarten. Eine Dorfkindheit* (*The Princess in the Herb Garden. A Village Childhood*, Ammann, 2000; Piper Verlag, Munich, 2003); a volume of essays, *Textur. Reden und Aufsätze.* (*Texture. Speeches and Essays*, Ammann, 1998), and the prose book *Der Berg über der Stadt. Zwischen Goethe und Buchenwald.* (*The Mountain Above the Town. Between Goethe and Buchenwald.* Ammann, 2003). Amongst the many volumes he has edited, or co-edited, is *Stimmen aus Buchenwald. Ein Lesebuch* (*Voices from Buchenwald. A Reader,* Wallstein Verlag, Göttingen, 2002).

## fledermausabend

in betrachtung des himmels, sterne
noch nicht im geschirr, ein senken
und sinken, als es schon dämmert,
zwischen abend und nacht stehn,
auf einer terrasse, die uns trägt,
fremd und verwundert über das bildnis,
das der andere himmel zur ansicht
ausrollt, schattenhaft huscht es
nachthin und schwirrt, war es ein
luftzug im dunkelnden licht, fleder-
mausabend, hier holt sie mich ein,
umkreist mich die kindheit, schwarz-
geflügelte wesen, abendfrieden,
inszeniert von langer hand,
tagwerk bis in die nacht hinein,
drei kühe im gras, ein bauer mit
schemel und melkeimer, aufschäumendes
abendgemelk, nicht aufzuhalten
das fußfällige dunkel, soll ich ihm
beipflichten, wenn es die erde berührt?
fledermausabend, bald schon gestirnt.

*eve of the bat*


watching the sky, stars
not yet arrayed, a setting
and sinking, dusk there already,
between evening and night,
as we lean on the terrace
strange and bewildered by the tableau
unfolding before our eyes in
another sky, shadowy flitting
nightwards it swishes, was it a
draught in the dimming light, eve
of the bat, my childhood encircles me,
catches up with me, black-
winged creatures, peace of evening,
a scene set from long before,
day's work lasting into night,
three cows at grass, a farmer with
milking-stool and pail, the frothy
evening's milking, no holding back
the footfall of darkness, should I go
along with it, when it touches the earth?
eve of the bat, soon turned to stars.

## schwarzer freitag

die bräuche der zunft hiessen ihn wandern,
unruhe trieb ihn zu fuß bis Paris,
entlaufener tischlergeselle, einen krieg lang
verschollen, wars in Abu Telfan? Saß er
in Tumorkieland gefangen? São Paulo hieß
die stadt, wie zu lesen, eine karte aus Chicago,
erdbewohner, weltbefahrner globetrotter,
Deutscher Club Pretoria, hobel, zollstock
und auch wasserwaage hoch in ehren jedes werkzeug,
doch beiseite von dem holz auf aktien
umgesattelt, abenteurer, der das märchen
hans im glück sich selber vorgespielt, gang
zur börse hieß fortan sein tagewerk, nur
auf gold gesetzt, hoch gepokert, fieberhaft,
glück im spiel, ein vermögen, märchenhaft,
einmal will ich millionär sein, bauernhöfe
kaufen, Steinbachs ganze armutei, goldner boden,
alles lug und trug, schwarzer freitag
in Pretoria, sturz ins bodenlose nichts,
geld und den verstand verloren, lästiges subjekt,
völlig unvermögend, ab nach Deutschland
rückkehr des verlornen sohnes, gar nicht
märchenhaft: Bremen, Harrassprung, Hochweitzschen,
tief in Sachsen, doch jetzt geistverstört,
wirre reden, nur noch manchmal blitzt es auf
in den tiraden, wenn es ihm die zunge überschlägt,
tief gekränkt, jede woche einen brief an Adolf
Hitler, jedes wort ein vorwurf, petitionen ohne
echo, schrieb sich noch die finger wund: ich bin
widerrechtlich eingesperrt, was mich höchst empört,
edle tischmanieren, wie sie gang und gäbe waren
im Deutschen Club, gehn den leuten ab in dieser
anstalt, in Pretoria war ich geachtet, tadellose
kleidung, maßgeschneidert, fast zum krösus

## black friday

the custom of the guild demanded he travel;
restless he set off to walk to Paris,
run-away journeyman, long reported missing,
was it in Abu Telfan? Imprisoned in
Tumorkieland? São Paulo the name
of the city according to a card from Chicago.
earthdweller, world-traveller, globetrotter,
the German Club Pretoria, plane and rule,
even spirit-level, every tool respected,
but, as it happened, from woodwork
he changed direction into playing the stockmarket,
an adventurer, who saw himself
as Lucky Hans in the fairy tale, went
to the stock-exchange as his daily task,
betting on gold alone, playing high stakes,
feverish luck in gambling, a fortune,
fairy-tale fashion, 'when I'm a millionaire,'
to buy up farms, impoverished Steinbach,
walk on gold, all lying and deceiving,
black friday in Pretoria, fell into a bottomless pit,
lost his money and his reason, tiresome fellow,
completely destitute, back to Germany,
return of the prodigal son, far from fairy-tale:
Bremen, Harrassprung, Hochweitzschen,
deepest Saxony, but now disturbed in mind,
speaking like a lunatic, but sometimes flashing out
in tirades when his tongue ran away with him,
deeply offended, every week a letter to Adolf
Hitler, every word a reproach, petitions
without answer, wrote his fingers to the bone:
I was unjustly imprisoned, what enrages me most
with my perfect etiquette as was observed
at the German Club, is the complete lack
of manners in this institution,

aufgestiegen, als ich mithielt mit den männern,
die um das geheimnis wussten, wie man gold
zu gelde macht, steilstieg tief von unten
aus dem lehm, steilsturz von hoch oben, wo
die börsenjobber thronen. *lebensunwert* wär
sein leben, deutsche sprache ihm zum hohne,
ab nach Pirna auf den Sonnenstein, letzte
rechnung für die asche, ob er Hitler noch
verfluchte, als man ihn ins gas geschickt?

in Pretoria I was respected, spotless
clothes made to measure, became almost a croesus
as I kept up with men who knew
the secret of turning gold to money,
steep climb from deep under out of the clay,
steep fall from on high where
the stockbrokers are enthroned.
he was designated *not fit to live,*
scorned the German language,
off to Pirna and up into the Sonnenstein, the last
account was for his ashes, whether or not he still
cursed Hitler when he was sent to the ovens.

## augenweide

hinter der heckenzeile, die mich zerkratzt,
dicht in sich verkrallt, schäumt ein baum-
acker weißflächig auf, hoch ins wilde kraut
geschossen die umbelliferen, distelwolle
werden sie ernten, windgezupt,
herkulesstauden, brachial eingeschlichen,
die für nichtswürdig befundenen früchte
dem freien fall überlassen, ein fußgänger
in wilder flucht vor sich selbst
bis in die fermentierte ferne, ebenso
wahrnehmungsgetrübt ein andrer
unter der dunstglocke auf der suche
nach dem ferne land Elis
zum herdenreichen könig Augias.

*sight for sore eyes*

behind the lacerating hedgerow
froths an acre of white-edged woodland
thickly bunched together, umbellifers,
sprouted high into the wild scrub, thistledown
blown on the wind, harvest of this
herculean hogweed, insidiously infiltrated,
letting its good-for-nothing fruits fall free,
footing it in wild flight from itself
into the fecund distance, even as
another just as disturbed
beneath a cloud of pollution
went in search of the far land of Elis
to King Augeias of the many herds.

## stadtgang

alltäglich herdenweise berufstouristen,
nicht gut zu fuß, angeblich kulturbeflissen,
alles nur wegen Goethe, den die stadt
als lockvogel einsetzt, seit sie ihn
zum gipskopf verkommen ließ, während ich,
den stadtbilderklärern eilends entweichend,
den marktplatz querte, nach einer audienz
bei Herzogin Anna Amalia, stand einer,
touristisch gewaffnet im lodenlook
wie vernagelt mit seinem gerät, als ich
unversehens durch sein blickfeld lief,
das sehr begrenzt war, bekennerhaft
rief er mir nach: du linke sau, du!
sein zuspruch herzerfrischend bajuwarish,
wenn auch haarscharf angepöbelt, war
zu ehren ich gelangt völlig unverhofft
während eines stadtgangs, offen und ehrlich
das feindbild des mannes, nur des oberbayrischen
mächtig, der mich unverhohlen
als störenfried seines weltbildes entlarvte,
wie recht er doch hatte, mich links von sich
zu placieren.

## a walk through town

the daily herdlike procession of dedicated tourists
not good on their feet, evidently bent on culture,
all because of Goethe, whom the town set up
as a bait after they dumbed him down into
gypsum, while I hurried to avoid the town guides
as I crossed the market square, a man stood there,
after an audience with Duchess Anna Amalia,
rigged out in fashionable tourist gear,
as if nailed down by his equipment,
and just as I unawares walked through his field of vision
which was severely limited, he shouted
as if he recognised me: you lefty swine, you!
the style of address heartwarmingly bavarian
even if cutting abuse, was, as I came
to appreciate, completely unexpected
on an open and honourable walk through town,
thus cast as the man's arch enemy, though
speaking in only a broad alpine dialect,
he made no bones about unmasking me
as a hooligan and disturber of his kind
of peace, demonstrating thereby how
right he was to place me well
to the left of him.

## *der bärenhügel*

am Bärenhügel, wo ein wachtelpaar feldeinwärts rief,
durch ausgeglühten weizenschlag
lief im radgeleise mein sommertag,
am Bärenhügel, wo ein könig im silbersarg schlief.

am Bärenhügel, wo ein wachtelpaar feldeinwärts schlug,
umkreisten den ringwall zwölf standhafte linden,
ihren eignen schatten unterm laubdach zu finden,
am Bärenhügel, wo die sage einen könig zu grabe trug.

am Bärenhügel, wo ein wachtelpaar feldeinwärts schwirrte,
glänzte herauf, getroffen vom dunstenden licht,
einer flußlandschaft durchgrüntes auengesicht,
am Bärenhügel, wo des königs geschmeide im silbersarg klirrte.

am Bärenhügel, wo der wachtelschlag feldeinwärts hallt',
quert ich einen verschrotteten eisenbahnstrang,
der in weit geschwungnem bogen den berg bezwang,
vom Bärenhügel hinüber zur endstation Buchenwald.

*the barren hill*


a pair of quails cried downfield over the barren hill,
my summer day softly wheeling
through harvest time and the gleaning
where a king in a silver coffin lay asleep on the barren hill.

a pair of quails beat downfield over the barren hill,
twelve steadfast limes encircled the circling wall
to find where beneath the leaves their shadows fall
as legend bore a king to his grave upon the barren hill.

a pair of quails whirred downfield over the barren hill,
woods and water-meadows green on green
reflect a thinning light, a fading gleam;
his silver coffin clanked with jewels for the king on the barren hill.

on the barren hill downfield drumming of quails resounded;
I crossed over a disused railway line
that curved round into the far mountain
from the barren hill and beyond to terminus Buchenwald.

# UTA MAUERSBERGER

Uta Mauersberger was born in 1952 in Bernburg, Saxony-Anhalt. She spent her schooldays in Halle, and then studied librarianship in Berlin, before moving first to Cottbus and then to her present home in the city of Leipzig.

She is best-known as an author of children's books but published two well-received collections of poetry in the GDR period, *Balladen. Lieder. Gedichte.* (*Ballads. Songs. Poems.* Verlag Neues Leben, (East) Berlin, 1983) and *Rattenschwanz – Gedichte* (*Rat's Tail – Poems*, Verlag Neues Leben, 1989). Her poetry has not been published since 1989.

*Leipzig, September 1989*

Unterwegs sein. Verstehen lernen, was das Auge sieht.
Mauern beginnen zu wachsen oder fallen ein. Vorhänge seufzen.
Müllstäubchen tanzen im gestreiften Sonnenlicht.
Es ist Tag geworden.
Staubsauger saugen die Trümmer ein.

Toilettengesang! Als Fremde fortgehn mit dem Treppengeländer.
Gras graut. Wind hockt hinterm Kohlestaubhügel.
Du kämmst deinen Bart, ich halte mich sauber.
Nun wollen wir
die Türen einrennen im Herzen der Unmöglichkeit.

Aber die Strasse blendet. Frauenmund hat Gold im Haar.
Mein Kopf lässt mich im Stich. Sensenmann schlägt nach der Stunde.
Das Morgenlicht arbeitet die Schatten heraus.
Unsereins grüßt,
aber der Schatten antwortet nicht.

Dann wandern die Teppiche, dann flieht das Geschirr.
Dann enden die Rosen, dann dämmern die Türen. Dann haben die
Bauarbeiter mit fehlenden Elementen zu kämpfen.
Dann dreh ich mich dreimal um.
Dumm.

Nachbarn, verkleidet, spielen Napoleons Haufen.
Preußische Landwehrmänner erwarten die Strassenbahn. Ein Sachse
schläft im Stehen. Kampfflugzeuge jagen über den Himmel.
Das Spiel namens MENSCH AUF ERDEN tobt neben mir im
                                                    Klettergerüst.
Aber mein Tag ist gelaufen. Könnt ich doch springen!

Ach könnt ich über meinen Schatten springen!

## Leipzig, September 1989

We're on the way. Learn to understand what you see.
Walls expand or fall in. Curtains are sighing.
Dust is dancing in slanting sunlight.
Day has come.
Vacuums clean up the rubble.

Toilets singing! Strangers depart with the carved banisters.
Grass turns gray. Gusts of wind squat behind the coal dust.
You comb your beard. I make myself presentable.
Now we want
to batter through doors to reach the impossible.

But the streets are dazzling. A woman speaks with gold in her hair.
My head fails me. The hour of the grim reaper has struck.
Morning light is delineating shadows.
We greet each other
but the shadow makes no reply.

Then carpets walk, then dishes fly.
Then roses droop, then doors darken, then builders
have to make bricks without straw.
Then I turn round three times like a dervish.
Foolish.

Neighbours, dressed-up, re-enact Napoleon's gang.
Prussian homeguards wait for the tram. A Saxon
sleeps standing up. Fighter planes chase across the sky.
The children play MAN ON EARTH wildly beside me.
But my day is done. If only I could leap!

Oh, if only I could leap over my shadow!

## Leipzig, September 1990

Ruft die Könige! Löscht das Licht.
Das Herz will ins Herz kommen, Ruhe haben.
Ich hole meinen Bruder aus dem Schrank
und lege Schmuck an.

Wege, von Worten geblasen.
Worte, umgaukelt von Kellnern.
Staub torkelt.
Steine singen mit Fensterscheiben.

Volksfest! Lustig Wind um Ecken schaufeln
und Palmen in die Trümmer tragen.
Missverständnisse halten auf ewig zusammen.
Gespenster hören sich beim Atmen zu.

## Leipzig, September 1990

Summon kings! Put out the light.
Heart will find heart and be at peace.
I bring my brother out of the closet
and put on my jewellery.

Words blow walk-ways into existence.
Words are minstrelled by waiters.
Dust staggers.
Stones sing along with window-panes.

Folk festival! They keenly shovel wind round corners
sweeping palm leaves into the rubble.
Misunderstandings stay bound together for ever.
Ghosts listen to each other breathing.

*Leipzig, September 1991*

Stein beknirscht Stein
und Mördergrube erwacht als Herz.
Auf meinem Fuß tanzt eine Litfaßsäule.
Dicker Hund schnüffelnd aus der Asche liest.

Und heute: wer teilt den Kopf mit mir?
Mein Schmuck sträubt goldene Stacheln.
Mein Licht, hinters Licht geführt,
liest aus der Kaffeetasse.

Noch einmal Wolken russischen
Parfüms, wallen auf und verduften.
Das Herdgas flattert, aber die Häuser
nehmen wieder ihren Platz ein.

*Leipzig, September 1991*


Stone grinds stone
and a worm-pit possesses the heart.
At my feet a dancing banner.
A fat dog snuffles for signs in the ashes.

And today: who shares my thoughts?
My jewellery bristles with golden spikes.
My light, led astray by its own light,
reads fortunes in coffee-cups.

Clouds of Russian perfume once more
waft up and dissolve.
The gas cooker splutters, but houses
take up their positions again.

*Leipzig, September 1992*

Mercedes klettert ins Balkengerüst
zu mir, wir feiern und ich
tanze mit zwölf Zehen an den Füßen
zu Vogelgezwitscher rückwärts

Kopfstand der Schornsteine,
aber nachwachsende Mauern.
Strassen, die wegrennen, aber Käsewolken.
Koffer überschlagen sich am Boden zu
stiller Andacht Dixi-Klo

Willkommen und Abschied
sprechen aus einem Munde
um mitzureden
und du mußt sehr feine Flügel haben

## Leipzig, September 1992

Mercedes climbs up the balustrade
to me, we celebrate and I
dance with twelve toes on my feet
backwards to the twitter of birds

Chimneys stand on their heads
but walls are growing again.
Streets race away but the stink remains.
Baggage turns somersaults on the ground
while I meditate O Portaloo

Welcome and farewell
speak from the same mouth
to communicate
and you must have very fine wings.

*Leipzig, September 1993*

Im Irrgarten winken Speisekarten
Blumen schmatzen
Polizisten singen an Bachs Grab

## Leipzig, September 1993

Menus flutter in the maze
flowers smack their lips
policemen sing at Bach's grave

## Vom Turm zu Babel überlebt die Besenkammer

Unbeleuchtete Worte rempeln die Wand, Staub steht auf und frisst sie.
Dazu trink ich stilles Wasser.

## From the Tower of Babel a Broom Cupboard Survives

Unlit words stagger against the wall; dust rises up and devours them.
I drink still water with it.

# ANDREAS REIMANN

Andreas Reimann was born in 1946. In 1953 his father, who had been editor of the newspaper *Leipziger Volkszeitung* and had been involved in the Berlin uprising, had to escape from the GDR and fled to the West. In 1954, after harassment from the authorities, his mother committed suicide; Andreas and his younger sister were placed in a children's home. In 1955 his father died in mysterious circumstances – most likely murdered by GDR agents, although this has never been proven.

From 1956 the children were looked after by their paternal grandmother in Leipzig until her death in 1968. In 1959 Reimann had his first poems published. From 1963 he was an apprentice typesetter, but in 1966 matriculated from the Leipzig Literature Institute. Early in 1967 he was released from military conscription after attempted suicide, but was arrested in 1968 for 'activities dangerous to the State' and imprisoned until the end of 1970.

After his release he worked in transport and as a bookkeeper. Two volumes of poetry were published in the 1970s, after which he suffered a further ban on publication, which was to last until the fall of the GDR régime in 1989. During this time Reimann collaborated with various singers and cabaret performers. After 1990 he published several books and in 1997 he received the Literary Promotion Prize (Literatur-Förderpreis). In 1999 he received a stipend from the State of Saxony and was honoured by the long-established Schiller Foundation. In 2000 he received the Leipzig Literature Award.

His collections of poems include *Der Olivenspiegel* (*The Olive Mirror*, Verlag Die Scheune, Dresden, 2003), *Die Männliche Zeitalter* (*The Masculine Age*, Konkursbuchverlag Claudia Gehrke, Tübingen, 2001), *Das Sonettarium* (*The Sonnetarium*, Connewitzer Verlagsbuchhandlung, Leipzig, 1995), *Leipziger Allerlei, Allerlei Leipzig* (*Leipzig Every Which Way*, Forum Verlag, Leipzig, 1993).

## Gedicht des Gedichts

Bewirkungslose sind wir allesamt:
ein knapper regen, der das gras nicht labt.
Ach, armer dichter, grau und abgeschabt,
der aus dem lande aberglauben stammt:

gedichte gehn zunichte, ehe sie
auf dem papier zum wort geronnen sind.
Die besten verse sind ein stotterwind,
wenn man sie misst an einem schmerz, der nie

zur sprache kommt. Die liebe und der tod
sind anzudeuten, doch zu sagen nicht:
bewirkungslose sind wir allesamt...

Denn das gedicht, zu glanz und klang verdammt,
ist fast ein schweigen, wenn der dornbusch loht.
Und stirbt's, stirbt scheinbar nichts als ein gedicht.

## Poem About Poetry

We are so altogether purposeless:
a meagre rain that fails to soak the grass.
Poor poet, patched-up, shabby, colourless,
from the land of Make-Believe-Romance.

Poems come to nothing long before
they scramble into words on the paper.
The best, a gust, a stammer, nothing more,
if measured with a suffering that never

reaches speech. We allude to love and death
yet these may not be mentioned: it is thus
we are so altogether purposeless.

The poem, condemned to seem but pomp and fuss,
is almost silence – like the burning bush –
and dying, just a poem come to grief.

## Orpheus an Euridike

Klag länger nicht. Schon als ich wußte, wie
ich dich aus deinem tod erlösen könnte,
wußt ich dich ganz verloren in dein ende,
denn götter zeigen gnade nur, wenn sie
uns gründlich wissen. Nichts als zeitvertreib:
sie lassen dich aus ihrer dunkelzelle
barmherzig in des tages schreckenshelle
und unterm räderrolln zerbricht dein leib.

Wär schwerer meine prüfung, wär sie leicht.
Ich aber kann, du weißt es, nicht nicht sehn,
so wußt ich, daß wir zugrunde gehen,
wie's götter wußten, und es ist erreicht.

Ich sah dich gegen jene hoffnung an,
daß irgendeiner je entkommen kann.

## Orpheus to Euridice

No more complaint. As soon as first I knew
that I could free you from your death I knew
you would be lost completely in the end:
the gods will only grace to us extend
when they know us throughly. Nothing for fun:
they let you wander forth from their dark prison
with mercy into day's appalling hell
to crush your body underneath their wheel.

Had my trial been harder, it were easy;
you know how I can't possibly not see,
and so I knew that we would be interred
as knew the gods and as has now occurred.

I looked at you against that very hope
that death would ever let someone escape.

## Neuzeit

O zeit, O zeit, in der ein traum des knaben
im schimmel-alter doch noch sich erfüllte
und nach der plage mit den küchenschaben
ihn wundersam der freiheits-strom umgüllte!

Statt ekler schaben stelzen edle raben
durch mein gefild. – Es ist nicht tag, nicht nacht.
Was dämmert, nennt man staat. – O zeit der gaben:
der traum ward wahr! – Um die verlorne schlacht

nun grämt euch nicht, die ihr aus morschen waben
in etwas sprühlicht neulich ausgeschwärmt,
ihr bienchen all! Wahr ward der traum des knaben.
Die freiheit nicht, nur ihr guckt so verhärmt.

Doch glück ist ohne trauer nicht zu haben:
der traum ward wahr.
Und somit auch begraben.

## The New Era

Oh time, oh time, in which a young boy's dream
in mildewed age at last has been fulfilled
and he's engulfed in freedom's wondrous stream
now that the plague of vermin is dispelled.

Instead of filthy roaches, noble ravens
strut through my fields. It's neither day nor night.
The state, so-called, is dawning; gifts are given:
the dream came true! – and as for that lost fight

you do not need to grieve, as you swarm forth
anew from rotten hives in shining sprays –
all little bees! Came true the dream of youth.
Freedom's unscathed, it's you who bear the scars.

Yet happiness is never without grief:
the dream came true.
                    And thus it meets its death.

# Friedhof

Der stelen katholisches weiß
überleuchtet die gräber so rein,
daß eine sehnsucht nach außer der welt
ins herbstliche sommert.

Ich glaube, hier ist den toten
der marmor leicht. Und das regengespräch
verständlich ihnen wie ein
grüngebliebenes wort.

Aus der behausung zypresse
flügelt schweigend ein käuzchen.
Nach wem solls denn rufen? Wir sind schon fast da,
hier, wo aus leibern die lilien blühn,
während die seelen im sonnenschein
mit alten weiblein vertraulich plaudern
über die kabeljaupreise
und über der lebenden ahnungen vom
anderswo, das die sich vorstellen freilich
wie eine grappa-und-einhorn-taverne,
in die ich nun einkehren werde:

durch eine stunde im kreise der toten
wiederbelebt.

## Graveyard

Stele in catholic white
illumine the graves so purely
that a yearning for the beyond
summers to autumn.

I believe the marble is light
here for the dead and they
understand the chatter of rain
like an evergreen word.

An owl flies silently out
from the shelter of cypresses.
For whom is it calling? We are still here – just,
here, where lilies blossom from corpses,
while souls gossip confidingly
in the sunshine with little old women
about the price of cod or
about live presentiments from
somewhere else, that they clearly see
like a grappa and unicorn tavern
where I shall now be going:

brought back to life from an hour
in the company of the dead.

## Wiederholen

Nicht um mich auszuruhn: um aufzuwachen:

einmal im jahr, wenn mit honig gefüllt
und reif wie entscheidungen fallen die feigen
und in den trauben der wein
sich vorbereitet, uns tanzen zu lehren;

einmal im jahr, wenn ich weigere mich
auf zungen zu hören, die knarren
wie dürstende dielen, während bei nah
vokale mundrund kollern hinab
die schmalen gassen zum markt;

einmal im jahr, wenn der berg schon gelassen
empfängt die zerdrieselten, sirrenden schwärme
des unsteten schnees,
während noch rot die granatäpfel kochen
im laubkorb der bäume am ufer des sees,

am steinreichen ufer des sees
einmal, noch einmal im jahr...

Und in den wassern olivenblätter: forellen.

Unbemüht treibt
der fisch in der strömung.
Und es schwimmet der fisch in die flut
eine strömung hinein.

## Returning Again

Not for me to sleep, but to reawaken:

once a year when, figs are falling,
honey-filled and ripe as decisions,
when grapes ferment into wine
to teach us to dance;

once a year when I refuse to listen
to tongues that creak like thirsty floorboards
while approximate vowels nearby go
roundmouthed rolling down
alleyways to market.

Once a year when snow breaks loose
from the mountain and in a seething
rapture, fragments, melts, while
pomegranates redden and ripen
in a cradle of trees beside the lake,

on the lakeshore, rich with pebbles,
once, but once a year...

And olive leaves in the water: rainbow trout.

Fish swim effortlessly
in the stream
and are borne by the current
out into the main.

## Widerrufliche Ermutigung

Mutter ist nicht aus der wohnung gegangen.
Die pulsadern klafften, ihr leib
weiß wie die flagge, die sie nicht zeigte:
ach, diese verwechslung von niederlage
und untergang, unwiderruflich. Und dann
vater ist nicht aus der wohnung gegangen,
sondern ins andere zimmer, es gingen
trunken die gäste, erdrosselt
fand ihn ein weib, doch nichts der ermittler.
Oder? Das fragezeichen
krümmt sich, ein rostender nagel,
der nicht in den sargdeckel will.

Der untergang aber ist aller
tage ende noch lange nicht.

Grossmutter zog von den gruben weg
die kinder. Sie ging aus der wohnung nicht
nochmals. Man hat sie hinausgetragen
und in der wiese ein loch gegraben
und sie mit erde bedeckt.

Tiefer nicht sinken die toten, und nicht
die gestorbenen jahre,
sondern der hügel, geräumt von den kränzen
wieder und wieder, wölbt sich zum berg.

Wer draufsteht, und folglich dem denkmal
macht streitig sein plätzchen, gewinnt
die übersicht, wenn auch der anblick von droben
ihm seine aussicht vergällt.

Tja, schwer ist das leben, denk ich da, aber:
das schwerste ist sterben. Und das
kann schließlich jeder.

## Uncalled-for Encouragement

Mother did not go out of the house.
Her arteries slit, her body white
as the flag she did not wave.
Oh irrevocable this confusion
between defeat and destruction. And then
father did not go out of the house
but into another room, drunken guests
had departed, a woman found him strangled,
but the inspector found nothing.
Or did he? The question mark
is crooked, a rusty nail
that won't go into the coffin.

Destruction though is far
from being the end of the story.

Grandmother pulled the children from the abyss.
Once again, she did not go out of the house.
She was carried out, a hole dug
in the field where she
was covered with earth.

The dead do not sink deeper
nor the years that have died,
but the mound, again and again
adorned with wreaths, has grown to a hill.

If you stand upon it and mark
your narrow plot behind the memorial,
you'll have a view, an overview,
but it is not a pleasant one.

Yes, life is hard I think, but
dying is the hardest. And that
we can all achieve in the end.

## Utopia

Wenn in die märkische wüste der leguan heimkehrt,
ein seltsamer sandfisch, und wir uns in dörrobst verwandeln,
da unserer selbst wir uns niemals erbarmten: wie klar
wird dann der frieden sein endlich! aus allen verstecken
züngelt, zunächst nur sehr zögerlich, zierlich das gras,
ein schachtelhalmwald überwächst die bedrohlichen dome...

Und gott wird vielleicht aus dem lehm, drin die schöpfungen ruhn,
nicht nochmals formen den größenwahn.

Es werden nicht wir sein, die, was wir voraussehn, erblicken.

Doch über den heimgekehrten gewässern
werden silbrig die mücken kichern.
Und alle natur
         wird unsern verlust –
                  wenn überhaupt –
vermutlich bemerken:

mit großer erleichterung.

## Utopia

When the iguana returns to the Brandenburg wastes,
a strange amphibian, and we change into dried fruit –
for we never had pity on ourselves – how clear
then will peace be at last! from every hiding-place
grass will delicately, at first oh so hesitantly,
put out its tongue; a forest of ferns will grow over
the oppressive cathedrals...

and, from the clay where the creatures rest, god
will perhaps not ever again give form to the megalomaniac.

We shall not be the ones who will see this vision.

Yet the silvery midges will titter
upon the returning waters
and the whole of nature
                    will presumably
                              notice our disappearance,
if at all,

with the utmost relief.

# THOMAS ROSENLÖCHER

Thomas Rosenlöcher was born in 1947 in Dresden and came to literature by a roundabout route. He began in trade, and then completed his military service in the Nationale Volksarmee (National People's Army). After military service he completed his Abitur (high-school graduation certificate) in Freiberg, after which he spent four years at the Dresden Technical University. Upon graduating he became a labour economist, but had already begun writing. From 1976 to 1979 he studied at the Johannes R. Becher Literary Institute in Leipzig. After leaving the Institute he worked at the Dresden Youth Theatre and regularly translated poetry. Since 1983 he has been a freelance writer and lives near Dresden.

His own collections of poems were successful, selling out in the GDR, and he gained a wider public, above all in the West, with his book *Die verkauften Pflastersteine. Dresdener Tagebuch (Sold Cobblestones. Dresden Diary*, Suhrkamp Verlag, Frankfurt, 1990).

His more recent publications include *Am Wegrand steht Apollo (By the Wayside Stands Apollo*, Insel Verlag, Frankfurt & Leipzig, 2001), *Ich sitze in Sachsen und schau in den Schnee (I sit in Saxony and look at the Snow*, Suhrkamp, Frankfurt, 1998) and *Die Dresdener Kunstausübung (The Practice of Art in Dresden*, Suhrkamp, 1997).

The poems featured here are drawn from the book *Am Wegrand steht Apollo*; they were inspired by a residency that the poet had at Wiepersdorf, the former home and estate of Achim von Arnim, one of the key writers of 19th-century German Romanticism.

Geh in Gedanken mit Arnim spazieren.
Angeberisch weiß starrt das Schloss durch die Bäume.
An der Terrasse steht: Zutritt nur
für Künstlerhausgäste. Kopfschüttelnd legt er
die Hand an den Stamm der noch von ihm gepflanzten
riesigen Eiche, durchs kahle Geäst
schiebt sich ein Nörgeln in Richtung Berlin.
Das ist ein Flugzeug, erläutere ich –
Welches Jahrhundert haben wir jetzt? –
Das Übernächste – Ihm scheint es recht.
Erst wer vergessen ist, kann wieder sein,
was er gewesen war, um zu werden.
Die Arnimschen Gräber sparen wir uns.

In imagination go walking with Arnim.
The castle stares garish white through the trees.
On the terrace it says: *Admission only*
*to artists-in-residence.* Shaking his head
he places his hand on the trunk
of the great oak he planted himself.
A droning that sounds in the Berlin direction
intrudes between bare branches. I explain –
that's an aeroplane. – What century is it now? –
The next but one – He seems to agree.
Only the forgotten can again be
what they were, to go on becoming.
Let us avoid the graves of the Arnims.

# Zerwürfnis

Auf dem Weg ein flaches Häufchen Laub.
Das, eben noch schlummernd, irrwitzig rasselnd,
von aussen nach innen um sich selber rannte.
Und, halbhoch aufflatternd, mir entgegensprang: Ein
fauchendes Flämmlein. Rettete mich
grad noch auf die Steinbank. Da aber nahm es,
mit fingrigen Blättern ans Brillenglas klopfend,
auf meinem Schoß Platz. Bettina! sprach ich.
Ich bin doch kein Goethe! Zurückprallend warf es
sich zwischen die Bäume und sah mich im Umkreis
aus dunklen Laubaugen todtraurig an. –
Schritt hierauf den Arm hinterrücks angewinkelt
durchaus nach der Art des Geheimen Rats weiter.
Aber das Windrad, das kollernd vorbeisprang,
würdigte mich keines Blicks.

## Quarrel

On the path a shallow pile of leaves
which even in slumber rustled and coiled
madly around and inward upon itself.
A thin hissing flame sprang up at me
waist high, so that I jumped
to safety on a stone bench.
But then, hitting my glasses with leafy fingers
it settled right in my lap. Bettina! I shouted,
I am no Goethe! It reared back
and plunged into the trees whence it watched me
dark-eyed from encircling foliage, sad as death.
I strode forward, my arms tucked behind
in the manner of the Geheimrat.
But the whirler rolling right past me
took not the slightest notice.

Die Gräber der Arnims umgittert.
Kein Blatt, keine Ranke. O Preußen.
Der Schritt knirscht auf dem Kies.

Einen Steinwurf weiter die Wagen
der immer noch Lebenden.
Matt schimmern Stoßstangen herüber.

Es gibt kein Erinnern. Nur dieses
Gegeneinander der Zeiten.
Kein Schritt kennt den anderen.

Aber der Wald ist ein eiserner Warter.
Und weiß den Weg in das Schloß.
Und wird in den Fenstern die Laubfahnen hissen.

Ja, auch die Lieben sind nur eine Zeit
vorausgefahrn auf dem Weg in die Zeit,
in der alle Zeiten ausruhn.

## The Graves of Achim and Bettina von Arnim

Iron railings enclose their graves.
Not a leaf, not a tendril. Oh Prussia.
Footsteps crunch on the gravel.

A stone's throw away the cars
of those who are still alive.
A dull shimmering of bumpers.

There is no remembering.
Only these conflicting times.
One step doesn't know the next.

But the woods are patient as iron.
They know their way into the castle
hoisting banners of leaves at the windows.

Yes, even loved-ones have gone ahead
for a time on the path into time
in which all times are at rest.

## Die Nachtigallenfrage

Gestern Geburtstag. Lag im Gras und schlief.
Da traten die Freunde von allen Seiten
an mich heran. Meisterchen, riefen sie.
Wir sind gekommen, dir zu gratulieren.
Wozu, dachte ich, wenn jedes Jahr bloß
wieder ein Jahr fehlt? Und rührte mich nicht,
bis sie verstummten. Friedemann, der Arzt ist,
legte mir lauschend den Kopf auf die Brust,
erhob sich und nickte: Es ist geschehn.
Er hatte noch viel vor, sprach Lühr
als Ortschronist. In den Zweigen ein feurig
klopfendes, tropfendes, schleifendes Singen.
Ob das eine Nachtigall war –
oder selbst jetzt bloß ein Sprosser?
Hätte das gern Ernst vom Fachverband
Sächsischer Ornithologen gefragt,
aber schon schritten sie plaudernd und lachend
über die Wiese. Erst jetzt sah ich dich.
Mann, wie du schwebtest zwischen den Männern!
Wartet, wie alt war ich heute geworden?
Wollte noch winken, der Arm viel zu schwer.

## The Nightingale Question

My birthday yesterday. Slept on the grass.
Then my friends came upon me from every
direction and shouted, little master,
we've come along to congratulate you.
What for, I thought to myself, when each year
only leaves one year less? I didn't move
until they were quiet. Friedemann, a doctor
put his head to my chest and listened,
looked up and nodded: it's stopped. He still has
many plans, said Luhr, the local historian.
Among the branches I heard a passionate,
rhythmical, liquid, throaty singing.
Could it be a nightingale –
or just some kind of artful thrush?
I'd have asked Ernst from the Association
of Saxon Ornithologists, but they
were already striding away over
the field, chatting and laughing. It was just
then I caught sight of you. Woman, how you
floated and wafted amongst all those men!
Wait a moment, how old was I today?
I wanted to wave; my arm weighed too much.

# Glocken

Im Holzgestühl bei der Kapelle
die beiden Glocken. Selbst an Sonntagen
kaum noch geläutet, und wenn, nur solange,
bis die letzten Huscheln der Christenheit
durch die Pforte geschlüpft sind. Doch heute ist Mittwoch.
Und sie läuten und läuten. Was ist denn da los?
Bescheid weiß Frau Schmidt. Was schon? Eine alte
Frau ist gestorben. Da läuten sie immer,
zwei Mann im Wechsel, zwei volle Stunden.
Wir sterben alle. Erst wir, die Alten,
doch dann sind gleich Sie dran. Wissen Sie das nicht?
Doch, doch, sage ich. Kein schlechter Gedanke,
daß dich, wenn du tot bist, zwei Stunden lang
ein eiserner Klöppel nochmal überdenkt.

*Bells*

Two bells in the wooden belfry of the chapel.
Hardly rung now even on Sundays, and then
just for as long as it takes for the last trace
of Christendom to be smuggled
through the doors. But today is Wednesday
and they keep on pealing and pealing.
Whatever is it? Frau Schmidt will know.
An old woman has died. So two men take turns
to keep the bells ringing for two whole hours.
We all of us die. First it is us, the aged,
but then it will all at once be your turn.
Don't you know that? Yes, of course, I say.
No bad thought though that an iron clapper
still keeps you in mind for two hours
after you die.

# ELMAR SCHENKEL

Elmar Schenkel was born in 1953 in Westphalia. He studied Philosophy, Art History and Sinology in Marburg and then Romance Languages & Literature, English Language & Literature and Japanology in Freiburg. He completed his doctorate in 1983 with a thesis on John Cowper Powys, and then a post-doctoral thesis on modern British poetry in 1991, before becoming a Professor. He has taught at the Universities of Freiburg, Konstanz and Tübingen and has been a Visiting Professor at the University of Massachusetts, Amherst. He is currently Professor of English Literature at the University of Leipzig.

He has been active as a writer and translator since 1975 and has edited or co-edited *Das Nachtcafé – Zeitschrift für Literatur, Flugasche* and *Chelsea Hotel Magazine*. He writes regularly for the *Frankfurter Allgemeine Zeitung* and *Frankfurter Rundschau* newspapers, and is a member of the Advisory Board of *The Powys Journal*. His translations of British poets include Iain Crichton Smith, Basil Bunting (*Briggflatts*) and Ted Hughes (*Crow*).

His many publications include *Mauerrisse* (*Tears in the Wall*, prose), *Blaenau Ffestiniog* (short stories), *Blauverschiebung* (*Shifting Blue*, poetry), *Der Aufgefangene Fall* (*The Captured Fall*, essays) and the travel books *In Japan* and *Massachusetts*.

## Schule des Vergessens

In unserer Schule gibt es nur ein einiges Fach. Es heißt Vergessen. Von morgens früh bis mittags, dann ab drei wieder bis in den Abend üben wir dieses größte und schwierigste aller Fächer. Nach drei Jahren sind wir Schüler schon recht erfolgreich im Vergessen. Man lobt uns, wenn wir unsere Hefte nicht mehr mitbringen oder den Eingang nicht finden. Ja, sagt unser Dr Schneider, wenn ihr nicht mehr und mehr vergesst, dann bleibt alles so wie es ist. Wir lehren euch das Vergessen, damit etwas Neues passiert.

Unsere Lehrer sind wahre Meister ihres Faches. Man hat sie aus allen Landesteilen zusammengeholt und ihr Ruhm dringt bis ins ferne Ausland. Es sind Glanzlichter. Auf vielen Turnieren und Olympiaden des Vergessens haben sie ihre Fähigkeiten unter Beweis gestellt, und zahlreich sind die Auszeichnungen, die sie eingeheimst haben. Ihr Licht fällt auf uns.

Unser Lehrer für das Spezialgebiet Sprachenvergessen zum Beispiel hatte nur wenige Wochen dazu gebraucht, seine Muttersprache zu vergessen. In Fremdsprache machte er noch schneller. Heute ist er soweit, dass er mühelos drei Sprachen pro Tag vergessen kann. In dieser Hinsicht ist er schneller als der gefürchtete Meister von London, der dafür allerdings mehr Wörter pro Minute wegschaffen kann. Auf das Ganze kommt es an, ruft unser Lehrer immer.

Nicht weniger beeindruckend ist unsere Lehrerin für Geschichtsvergessen. Sie bringt uns bei, wie man in einer einzigen Stunde zwölf Kreuzzüge, dreiunddreißig Kanzler sowie ein tausendjähriges Reich vergessen kann. Manchmal ist es leichter, etwas Fernes und Schweres wegzuzaubern als etwas Nahes und Leichtes. Da hält sich ein Dunst, ein Schimmer, auch wenn wir schon stundenlang an der Substanz gearbeitet haben.

Warum gerade unsere Schule so erfolgreich ist, muss wohl mit ihrer speziellen Lage zu tun haben. Sie steht in Reudnitz, gleich neben einer gigantischen Brauerei. Ganz besonders zeigt sich der Erfolg unseres Lernens, wenn wir so manchen Morgen nicht mehr wissen, wozu es unsere Schule gibt und wo sie überhaupt steht. O ja, ich

## The School of Forgetting

There is only one subject in our school. It is called Forgetting.
From early morning to noon, then again from three till evening, we
practise this greatest and most difficult of disciplines. Within three
years we pupils become quite good at forgetting. We are praised
when we no longer remember to bring our jotters or cannot find
the way in. Indeed our Dr Schneider tells us, 'if you don't keep on
forgetting more and more, everything will stay the way it is. We
teach you to forget so that something new can happen'.

Our teachers really are masters of their art. They have been gathered
together from all over the country and are even famous abroad.
They are shining lights. They have had their abilities put to the test
at many a tournament, or Olympics even, for Forgetting and have
brought home numerous awards. Their light is shed on us.

Our teacher in the specialist area of Forgetting Language, for
instance, took only a few weeks to forget his mother tongue. With
foreign languages he was even speedier. Now he has reached the
point where he can effortlessly forget three languages a day. He is
faster in this respect than the eminent Professor from London, who,
however, can eliminate more words a minute. 'Completeness is what
we are aiming for', our teacher is always declaiming.

No less impressive is our instructress in Forgetting History. She is
teaching us how to forget twelve crusades, thirty-three chancellors
as well as an empire of a thousand years in a single hour. It's often
easier to magic away what is distant and heavy than what is near
and light, which will retain a haze, a shimmer, even when we have
struggled for hours with the substance.

The success of our school must have something to do with its
particular situation. It is in Reudnitz, right beside a gigantic brewery.
The outcome of our work is most clearly seen when we no longer
know the purpose of our school or, on many a morning, even where
it is. Oh yes, I vaguely remember we are fulfilling some important
task. Were it not for us everything would come to a stop and turn
to stone.

crinnere mich vage, wir erfüllen eine wichtige Aufgabe. Ohne uns bliebe alles stehen und würde zu Stein.

Manchmal studieren wir so intensiv, dass wir vergessen, was unser Fach eigentlich ist. Uns selbst vergessen wir andauernd, aber das ist nebensächlich. Wenn wir zu Hause ankommen, fällt es uns schwer, über unsere Erfolge zu berichten. Ich wundere mich überhaupt, dass ich diesen Bericht zustandebegracht habe.

Sometimes we concentrate so intensely we forget what our subject is. We continually forget ourselves, but that is beside the point. When we get home we find it difficult to relate our successes. What surprises me most of all is that I've completed this report.

## Die Unsichtbare Passage

Das Buch war fertig, doch da sagte jemand, wo ist hier eigentlich eine wirkliche Passage, durch die auch das Fussvolk hindurchgehen kann? Es ist doch die Stadt der Passagen, die du vor dir hast. Also: wo sind sie?

Gut, also wo sind sie? Ich dachte an die Passagen, die mir einfielen, Königshauspassage, Messehauspassage, Madlerpassage, und die überirdischen Tunnel, in denen die Läden wie Bälle hin-und hersprangen und auf- und zugingen wie Augenlider. In der einer war der Laden mit den Masken und den Reisen um die Welt in 80,000 Buchstaben, der mit den Fahnen und Bumerangs. Eines Tages wird jemand den Passagen-Bumerang erfinden, der mühelos durch alle Gänge fliegt und nach einigen Stunden unerwartet wieder zurückkehrt. In der anderen klopfte das Meissener Porzellan nach unsichtbaren Rhythmen. Hier Lichthöfe, dort ein Glas gefangener Himmel, ein Himmel, der wie in einem Aquarium schwamm, ein Himmel, in dem die Fische Nester bauten. Ein gläserner Berg auch, über den die Butterfahrten ins Jenseits gingen. Ein Wink aus der Hölle, ein Duft aus dem periodischen System, eine Apotheke, in der man sich besoff. Ich war versucht, mich mit Wissen anzufüllen über die Kulturgeschichte der Passagen, aber es gibt Zeiten, da muss man sich dem Wissen verweigern und Gedanken nachgehen, die an kein Wissen gebunden sind. Also ging ich nicht in das Antiquariat, sondern zum Friseur und ließ mir eine Variante in die Haare schneiden und dachte an die zerfallenen, verschollenen Passagen, an die Läden, in denen immerzu Schokolade umgegossen wird vom Nikolaus ins Osterei und zurück. An bewegliche Läden, wie in dem Krimi vom wandernden Spielzeugladen, der an unvermuteten Plätzen auftauchte. Da war die Buchhandlung, von der am Ende nur noch eine drehbare Gebetssäule übrig blieb. Man musste eine Mark hineinwerfen, um ihren Drehschwung zu erhalten. Sie entwickelte sich mit der Zeit zu einem Talisman. Mit den rasch wachsenden Einkünften, die jeden Abend eingesammelt wurden, baute der Buchhändler neue und größere Glücksäulen in der ganzen Stadt und vergaß die Bücher. Eines Tages wurde er dem Rat der Stadt vorschlagen, ganz Leipzig auf eine große Drehscheibe zu montieren, auf die die Welt dann ihre Glückspfennige werfen konnte. Er war

## The Invisible Passage

The book was finished but someone was asking where there was a real passage for footfolk to go through. This is the City of Passages you see before you. Well, where are they?

Yes, well, where indeed? Memories of passages come to mind: Königshauspassage; Messehauspassage; Madlerpassage; the high level tunnel where shops bounced up and down like balls and opened and shut like eyelids. The shop with masks was in one of them and with journeys round the world in 80,000 alphabetical letters, the one with banners and boomerangs. One day someone will discover Boomerang lane, which flies on and on through all the wynds and unexpectedly returns a few hours later. In another Meissen china chinked to unseen rhythms. Here lighted courtyards, there a bit of heaven caught in glass, a heaven swimming in an aquarium, a heaven where fishes built nests. A glass mountain too, where day-trippers passed into the beyond. A hint from hell, an aroma from the periodic table, a chemist's shop where you got intoxicated.

I was tempted to find out about the cultural history of the passageways, but it was time to turn away from knowing and to turn towards thoughts that are not bound by fact. So I didn't go into the antiquarian bookshop but to the hairdresser and had a new haircut and thought about the demolished or missing passageways, about shops where chocolate is poured non-stop from Christmas to Easter and back; about exciting shops, like the wandering toyshop in the thriller, that turned up in unexpected places.

There was the bookshop where eventually nothing remained but a single revolving column of prayer. You threw a coin to set it spinning. In due course it became a talisman. With the rapid increase in customers who gathered of an evening, the bookdealer was able to build new and larger lucky pillars all over the city and to forget about books. One day he would propose to the City Fathers that the whole of Leipzig be assembled on a huge disc, where all the world could throw its lucky pennies. He was even ready to set up the first Demolition Team. This was just the beginning.

schon dabei, die ersten Abräumkommandos aufzustellen. Wir standen erst am Anfang.

Die Stadt war untertunnelt worden nach dem letzten Bürgerkrieg, so könnte jetzt eine weitere Geschichte anfangen, aber für Geschichten ist jetzt nicht mehr die Zeit. Auf die Öffnungen der Tunnel hatte man Zyklopensteine gesetzt, mit Fenstern, mit Gerüchen, mit Stoff und Schmuck und Spiegeln. An den Wänden bewegten sich die Schatten, Reste von Stummfilmen. Zyklopische Kameras überall in der Stadt, Völkerdenkmal, Siegerdenkmal, Verliererdenkmal, das neue Rathaus, das viel älter war als das alte. Die Geschichten, die sich aus den begehbaren Passagen ergeben, sind begrenzt. Unendlich aber jene, die sich über die unsichtbare Passage denken lassen. Das Zeitalter des Atomischen Gottes überstand sie nicht, obwohl hier der Monistenbund regelmäßig seine Treffen abgehalten hatte. Ich weiß nur, dass eine Uhr in ihr hing. Diese erste überdachte Ladenstrasse der Stadt wurde 1873 erbaut. Jetzt ist dort ein Fleck Wiese, Hundescheisse, Telekom, ein Graffiti, eine lose Sicherung. Die Commerzbank zeigt ihre goldenen Zähne in der Sonne. Gelegentlich tauchen die fliegenden Händler auf, mit Würstchen, polnischem Schmuck und Schals aus Indien. Im Sommer ist mit Gitarren zu rechnen. Wann hörte die Uhr in der Steckerpassage auf zu ticken. Zwei Augen ziehen ziellos durch die Stadt, sie heißen Wann und Wo. Wenn sie sich treffen, was vorkommt, entsteht ein Gesicht, manchmal auch eine Passage.

After the last Civil War tunnels were built under the city. A new story could begin here. But storytime is over. Display fronts with windows, perfumes, materials, jewelry and mirrors had been placed like giant rocks at the entrances to the tunnels. Shadows and excerpts from silent films flickered on the walls. All over the city there were huge cameras focusing on memorials to the people, monuments to victory, monuments to defeat, the new City Hall that was much older than the old one.

The stories connected with these usable passages can be numbered, whereas those connected with the invisible passage are innumerable. It did not survive the age of the atomic god, although this is where the Monist group regularly held meetings. I know only that a clock hung there. This first covered shopping street in the city was built in 1873. Now there's a patch of grass, dogshit, telecable, a graffiti, a loose fuse. The Commerzbank displays its golden teeth in the sun. Hurrying merchants appear now and then with little sausages, Polish jewelry and Indian shawls. In the summer you can expect guitars. When did the clock stop ticking in the Steckner Passage? Two eyes, called When and Where, wander aimlessly through the city. If they meet, which can happen, a face emerges, sometimes even a passageway.

## Ende eines Spielplatzes

Wenn, am Morgen, auf den langen
unbekannten Wegen, das Glitzern
des unsichtbaren Sees im Rücken,
alles im Rücken, die Zeit
vorne schwindet, kein Polster mehr

für Zukunft, kein sanftes Hinein-
gleiten, nur Schärferwerden,
Kanten, geschliffen das Licht, die Tage – und

nun der Bagger, plötzlich, den vier
Hände dirigieren, vorzeitliches
Kletterrohr, verkratzte Rutsche im Griff,
das faulige Seil, Dinosaurier

sind es nicht, auch wenn. Letzte Verzerrung
im zerhämmerten Spiegel, bevor einer
die Scherben wegfegt, ins Loch,
ins Ich, die schwarze Kälte

der vergessenen Erde, mit Wurzeln
sträubt sich, strampelt
das herausgerissene Gerät, stumpf
schwebt das Rohr
in gelber Trauer fort.

## End of a Playground

When on long unfamiliar paths in the morning
glitter of the invisible lake
behind me, everything
behind me, time ahead
disappearing, no cushioning

for the future, no smooth
gliding into it, but getting sharper,
edges, polished light, days – and

suddenly now the digger
directed by four hands, takes control
of the prehistoric climbing frame,
though no dinosaur, with its scar-worn slide

and rotten rope. Last grimace
in the shattered mirror before someone
sweeps the fragments into a pit,
into the Ego, the black cold

of the forgotten earth, where
the ripped-out apparatus
wrestles and struggles with roots
as it is lifted, and glumly
sways away in yellow sadness.

## Blauverschiebung

Das wilde Licht
strömt von den Rändern her
und Blau liegt schief
verschiebt sich südlich. Zeit
zerbricht in Farbe neu.

Im Hause Ordnung
klappen Fenster auf:
Dreitausend Jahre sind
vergangen im Nu.
An die Tür Geschichte
klopft der Augenblick.

## Shifting Blue

Wild light
streams in from the edges
and blue lies squint
shifts to the south. Time
breaks up in colour new.

In the house of order
windows fly open:
three thousand years are
gone into the blue.
A moment is knocking
at the door of history.

# TESSA RANSFORD

# TESSA RANSFORD

## Good Friday, Leipzig 2002

Church bells keep on ringing
as I struggle with my grief.
'O Haupt voll Blut und Wunden'
as you composed it, Bach.

Nightlong translating poems
that hurt me to the bone
till frozen in my being
I fell asleep alone.
Life and death and children
our terror of rebirth:
what were you meaning, Jesus,
in that last sighing breath?

Like me, like any woman,
you sacrificed your life
but not to burden others
or drag them down to death,
rather as a freedom,
a shaking loose of bonds
that trap us in our safety
enchain us in our wrongs.

The streets are full of people
quietly on holiday
for shops are shut and markets
have put their wares away.

Sadness of children
I find it hard to see
and yet a child of sorrow
is crying still in me.
Much has been forgotten
that has formed what now I am
and what I become for others
is not subject to time.

My heartscape is sufficient
to hold and to release
what memory can't forgive
or hope rebuild in peace...
As we grope for resurrection
only one more day or
ten thousand years, it's with us,
haunts us, keeps us, everyway.

# Easter in Leipzig, 2003

*We came here to translate*
*and have been ourselves translated.*
*We came here to portray*
*and have seen ourselves portrayed.*

We had rational intentions:
Leipzig and Edinburgh after all
are cities of books and music and art.
But who has created these things?
They don't appear out of the dust
or from desks of bureaucrats.

Books are the printed flesh and blood
of those whose lives have written them.
Drawings are just that: drawn
out of human bodies that know
the terror of living. Music sets free
only those, like Bach, enslaved by it.

What is it we have to forget
in order to think in new ways
and what must we always remember
in order to know who we are?
Forgetting, a kind of death,
remembering, a resurrection.

*We came here to translate*
*and have felt ourselves translated*
out of our normal lives
wrenched from our children and friends
flung into this alembic of fire
and other people's lives.

*We came here to portray*
*and have seen ourselves portrayed*
through the eyes of poets and artists.
Amazed that we want to know them
they come to life before us, emerge
from their self-imposed resignations.

As we follow the golden thread
through the labyrinth of living
there is no art without adventure
no mercy without fire, no new
life without death and back to art:
*portrayal and translation.*

Printed in the United Kingdom
by Lightning Source UK Ltd.
128390UK00001B/31-48/A